THE CHRISTIAN

SABBATH

Don W. Robertson

New Creation Publications
P.O. Box 411, Coulterville, Illinois 62237

Dedicated to my wife, Cathy, who is a constant encourager, example of God's grace, and a dear friend in Christ.

Copyright © 2001
Don W. Robertson

All rights reserved. No part of this book may be reproduced in any form or by any means, except for brief quotations for the purpose of review, comment, or scholarship, without written permission from the author.

Unless otherwise stated, quotations from the Bible are taken from the Holy Bible: NEW INTERNATIONAL VERSION. Copyright © 1984 by the International Bible Society, New York. Published in Great Britain by the Press Syndicate of the University of Cambridge, and used by permission of Zondervan Publishing House, Grand Rapids, Michigan.

ISBN 0-9709072-0-6

Cover Photo: Copyright © 2001 Don W. Robertson and Corel.
All rights reserved

Printed in the U.S.A.
P.O. Box 411
Coulterville, Illinois 62237

TABLE OF CONTENTS

Foreword	4
Introduction	5
1. What Is the Sabbath?	6
2. Why Observe the Sabbath?	8
3. Which Day Is It?	13
4. How Should We Observe the Sabbath?	19
5. Summary	27
6. Study Questions	28
Index of Scripture	30
Works Cited	31

FOREWORD

The contents of this booklet first appeared as a seminary paper produced for a Christian Ethics Class at Covenant Theological Seminary in St. Louis, MO in 1993. There have been some modifications since then. As with anything written, there are sure to be more improvements in forthcoming editions. I only hope that this little booklet will encourage those who read it to better appreciate the Lord's Day as God has directed. From studying this subject, I have been challenged personally to better honor our Lord on Sunday and it is my desire that you, too, will likewise be encouraged to respect and honor the Lord on this holy day. We are living in a day in which the Christian Sabbath is too often being put aside and dishonored by not only the secular culture but even by those in the church. Having once served as a youth pastor, I noticed this unfortunate reality. Many young people were falling into the temptation to treat the Lord's Day just like any other day of the week with no regrets. God's people must learn what His Word has to say on this subject in order to model and teach this generation how it should respect the Sabbath. I look forward with optimism at what God can do regarding this matter if only His children will listen and obey. Please honestly consider God's Word on this subject and pray for the Lord's leading in your life to follow what He teaches you. All for the Glory of God.

Rev. Don W. Robertson, pastor
Grandcote Reformed Presbyterian Church
Coulterville, Illinois

INTRODUCTION

There are many confused and ambiguous understandings of the Sabbath amongst Christians today. Such interpretations have resulted in much misuse and lack of proper consideration of this most precious institution. Some would have us to believe that Sabbath day observance is not an issue that needs to be addressed today, but I must respectfully disagree. As a pastor, I have seen a growing apathetic attitude toward the Sabbath amongst believers, and it grieves my heart. Many dear pastors have expressed the same concern about this problem but don't seem to know what to do about it. They would love to again see an excitement and respect for the Christian Sabbath in the church and culture at large. As with any problem, the church has the best place to turn for a solution: the Word of God. If God's people will seek His Will on this matter and prayerfully request His grace to conform their lives to His Will, there can be again a renewed respect for the Lord's Day in the church.

I hope to help clear up some of the confusion surrounding the Sabbath by attempting to answer four important questions. Firstly, what is the Sabbath? Secondly, why is the Sabbath to be observed? Thirdly, when is the Sabbath to be observed? Lastly, how should we observe the Sabbath? By no means is this booklet an exhaustive treatment of the subject but it is a healthy beginning. It is my prayer that the Lord will greatly encourage, enlighten, and strengthen the faith of His people in the study of this vitally important subject: The Christian Sabbath.

1 | WHAT IS THE SABBATH?

Part of understanding the Sabbath is to consider its meaning in the Hebrew and Greek languages (which are the original languages of the Bible along with Aramaic). The Hebrew word for Sabbath is shabbat and when used as a verb means to "*cease, desist, and rest*" (Hamilton 902). When shabbat is used as a noun it most often refers to "*the day of rest, sabbath*" (Holladay 360) which is especially indicated in the Old Testament to be "the seventh day of the week" (Hamiltion 902). It should be noted that the New Testament word for Sabbath is sabbatōn and it is often defined as "the seventh day of the week in the Jewish calendar, marked by rest from work and by special religious ceremonies" (BAGD 739). The first occurrence of the concept of sabbath rest is found in Genesis 2:2-3. God is described as having completed His work of creation and then He 'rested' (shabbat) on the seventh day and made it 'holy' because "*He rested from all the work of creating that He had done*" (Gen. 2:3). At this point and time in history, the Sabbath day became **a special day of remembrance of God's creative work and man's utter dependence upon his Creator**. Surely God did not rest His omnipotent hand from holding together the Universe, for if He had, it would have collapsed in a moment. But God did cease from His colossal creative work of making the Universe and brought a climactic conclusion to His splendid art-work, thus resting on the Sabbath Day.

Some have argued that the Sabbath institution was not invoked until the administration of the Ten Commandments

(Ex. 20:8-11). Such an opinion seems quite contrary to scripture in that it fails to see the significance of God's making holy the seventh day in Genesis 2:2-3. We mustn't forget that the Sabbath Day was observed by the Hebrews prior to their receiving the Ten Commandments. For example, God had promised a double portion of manna in the wilderness on the sixth day so as to allow for the observing of the Sabbath: "*Six days you are to gather it, but on the seventh day, the Sabbath, there will not be any*" (Ex. 16:26). The Sabbath Day institution did not begin with the issuing of the fourth commandment on Mount Sinai (Ex. 20). By the time of Moses, the Sabbath was an already established "creation ordinance." With the institution of His written law, God was calling man to "remember the Sabbath Day" and therefore keep it as it was originally intended to be kept (Rayburn 73). God, with His own finger, inscribed upon the Ten Commandments His everlasting command for man to faithfully observe this precious institution. The Sabbath then obtained an explicit and abiding place in the moral law of God. So, therefore, we should accept the fact that the Sabbath Day had become an abiding institution in Genesis 2:2-3, which was more explicitly commanded in the decalogue (the Ten Commandments). Since we have established that the Sabbath was a divine institution, the question arises: why should man observe such an institution?

2 | WHY OBSERVE THE SABBATH?

There are a host of reasons why the Sabbath should be observed. After Christ and His disciples had picked some heads of grain in order to eat on the Sabbath, Christ defended His right to do so before the Pharisees by stating, "*The Sabbath was made for man, not man for the Sabbath*" (Mk. 2:27). Jesus was pointing out that the Sabbath was not meant to be a burden with legalistic requirements, but was **meant for man**. God didn't need the Sabbath; man needed it to be reminded of God. God knew that man needed the provision of the Sabbath to keep him from literally working himself to death and also to guard him from forgetting God's person and creative provisions. Another important reason to observe the Sabbath is **the example of God Himself** (Young 1042). If the Lord Himself saw fit to rest on the Sabbath, shouldn't we? Who are we to believe that our ability to endure the toils of labor can exceed the decision of God to rest? Even Christ observed the Sabbath Day. One author notes, "Christ Jesus during His earthly life was strictly obedient to the Sabbath law" (Rayburn 80). Suppose you were working in a garden under the management of an older and more experienced farmer. You notice the farmer has come to a complete halt in his work and has displayed an inviting spirit. Would you not join him in his shabbat (sabbath) or rather keep on working? To do the latter would be offensive to the invitation. In Ex. 20:8ff. God grounds His commandment to keep the Sabbath by resting on the seventh day and setting it apart as **"blessed and holy"**. If God considers the Sabbath Day blessed, shouldn't we?

The Sabbath is also to be observed because it is **a reminder of God's redemption** (Murray 258). We see in Deut. 5:15, that the Israelites are told to observe the Sabbath as a reminder of God's deliverance from their slavery in Egypt. The Israelites' 400 years of relentless labor had finally received a Sabbath rest by the hand of God. The redemption of the Israelites foreshadowed the future redemptive work of Jesus Christ on the behalf of all of humanity. All of redemptive history is climaxed in the resurrection of Jesus Christ. This redemptive picture is fully expressed in the Christian Sabbath in which the Christian is invoked to remember Christ's resurrection. In Christ, the Christian has received a greater deliverance, which is his deliverance from his slavery to sin. For Christ said, "*Take my yoke upon you and learn from me, for I am gentle and humble in heart, and you will find* **rest** *for your souls*" (Mt. 11:29). In our observance of the Sabbath Day we show forth our gratefulness and dependence upon God's redemptive work on our behalf.

Observation of the Sabbath also provides **humanitarian benefits**; "*that your manservant and your maidservant may rest, as you do*" (Dt. 5:12-15) (Rausch 964). It affords dependent laborers a day of rest. This is very applicable in our day and age where large corporations seek to squeeze all they can out of their workers. Blue laws have almost become non-existent, and businesses often fill every day with work regardless of anyone's Sabbath beliefs. As a public school teacher, my wife was periodically asked to attend work-related functions on the Sabbath, but thanks to some sensitivity from her principal, she was not forced into attending them. Many are not so fortunate. Frequently people have to make the decision to either work on the Sabbath or lose their job. This is a very serious matter.

Another reason to observe the Sabbath is because it is **a sign of the covenant** (Ex. 31:13,17; Ezk 20:12,20). It was a sign showing that God had made the Israelites holy (Ezk. 20:13), possibly just as He had made the Sabbath Day holy. It was a covenant reminder that God had created all things and had rested on the seventh day (Ex. 31:17). Probably most importantly it was a covenant reminder that the Lord was their God (Ezk. 20:20). For the Christian these truths are fulfilled in his belief in the person of Jesus Christ (Heb. 4:3). In Him, "rest" is found, but not yet fully realized as it will be in the future when the Christian leaves this world and goes to be with Christ in heaven (Rev. 14:13). There is a 'now but not yet' aspect to our present rest. The Sabbath Day best affords us the privilege to appreciate the 'now', and to eagerly expect the 'not yet' (Stibbs 1199).

John Calvin hesitated to make the Sabbath a legal requirement and supported the observation of it mainly on the basis of its **establishing order in the church** (Calvin 399). He saw the Sabbath as a "lawful selection that serves the peace of the Christian fellowship" (Calvin 399). Calvin makes a good point. Without the Sabbath Day, where would the unity of church assembly lie? Chaos would surely ensue. The body of Christ would greatly be hindered in its discovery, organization, and utilization of spiritual gifts for the edification of the church (1 Cor. 12;14). Corporate worship and fellowship is supported throughout the New Testament. For example, the writer of Hebrews states: *"Let us not give up meeting together, as some are in the habit of doing, but let us encourage one another--and all the more as you see the Day approaching"* (Heb. 10:26). But to make Calvin's thesis a sole reason for Sabbath Day observance seems to diminish the significance of its place in the Ten Commandments.

Perhaps, most importantly, the Sabbath Day has received a perpetual place within the moral law (Ex. 20:8-11; Deut. 5:12-15). It was and is **an eternal command of God**. Some theologians, especially dispensationalists, have postulated that the Sabbath Day was done away with as part of the moral law and therefore isn't applicable to the church (Lowery 649). But I contend that such a position should not be held because the Sabbath was not a ceremonial institution, but rather a perpetual institution. There were many ceremonial religious days that were under the theocracy of Israel which lost their binding effect; but the moral law expressed in the Ten Commandments never lost its obligatory standing.

The Ten Commandments are universal commandments that apply to all men in all cultures at all times. In addition, we should note that the Sabbath was already in place before the Jewish theocracy (Gen. 2:2-3) and therefore obligatory for all men regardless of nationality (Reymond 13). For even Jesus saw that the Sabbath was universally applicable in His statement: "*The Sabbath was made for **man**, not **man** for the Sabbath*" (Mk. 2:27). If we call the Sabbath Day a ceremonially discarded institution, do we not turn the Ten Commandments into the Nine Commandments? Or even worse, do we render suspect all the other commandments with such an interpretive method? One of the fundamental doctrines of the NT is the teaching that Christ did not come to do away with the law but to fulfill it (Mt. 5:17-20). The most sensible conclusion is that the Sabbath was and is a perpetual moral law awaiting its ultimate fulfillment when the believer will one day receive his eternal Sabbath in heaven. For this reason, we should not disregard its permanent place within the Ten Commandments (see fig. 1).

Figure 1

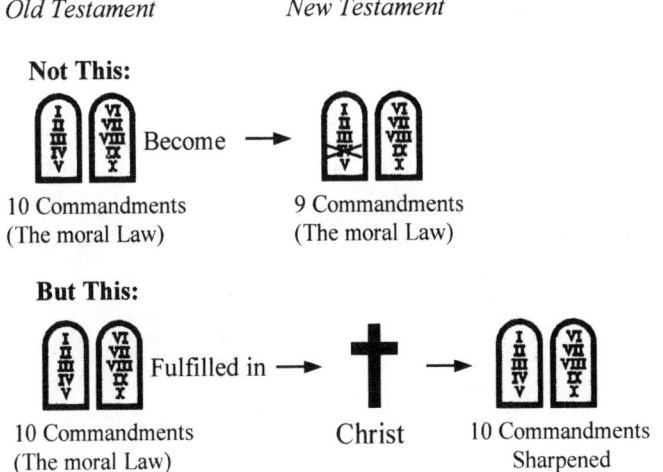

Lastly, we should consider the fact that **the wrath of God and His blessings** are closely tied to Sabbath observance. God's wrath was promised to the Israelites for their discontinuance and profanation of the Sabbath (Jer. 17:27; Ezek. 20:13). God's servants also got angry with Sabbath discontinuance and desecration. Nehemiah, an exemplary model of Sabbath obedience, warned the Israelites of God's wrath when they profaned the Sabbath; and he even promised to discipline them for their abuse of this holy day (Neh. 13:15-22). As a result of his warnings, the Israelites decided to straighten up their ways. When God's people observe His Sabbath, He blesses them. God promised that if both foreigners and Israelites observed the Sabbath, He would bless their obedience (Isa. 56:2-8; 58:13-14). While pastoring in Canada once, a dear retired Dutch immigrant farmer told me a marvelous story about such blessing. Egbert noted that he would not farm on Sunday during his years as a dairy farmer. His neighbors, however, who were not Christians, didn't observe the Sabbath but worked seven days a week. They couldn't understand why Egbert had such good crops year after year. Egbert knew the reason. He explained that his blessings had come from the Lord. This didn't mean, however, that he had no suffering in his life. His wife in fact suffered in her later years from crippling arthritis. But even in the midst of their suffering they still had a deep faith and joy in the Lord that was contagious. What greater gift can we expect for observing the Sabbath than the blessing of God? Nothing compares to His wonderful blessings. Now that we have established reasons to observe the Sabbath we must determine when the Sabbath is to be observed.

3 | WHICH DAY IS IT?

Some religious groups, such as the Seventh-Day Adventists, have taken the position that the Old Testament observation of the Sabbath on the seventh day should still be observed. Such persons are sometimes called **strict** or **literal sabbatarians** because they view the 7th day (Saturday) as the only day in which to fulfill the Sabbath law (Harm 963). Thus, they are very adamant that the Sabbath should be observed on Saturday rather than Sunday. One church historian provides helpful insights into understanding their position. Harm says, "Their arguments for the universally binding character of the sabbath law are these: it (1) is part of the moral law, (2) was given at the creation, and (3) was not abrogated in the NT. Some Adventists see in Sunday observance a fulfillment of the prophecy (Rev. 14:9ff.) which states that deluded mankind will be forced to accept the mark of the beast (Sunday observance) in order to survive during the days prior to Christ's second advent" (Harm 963). Some of the points of this view are correct, especially that the Sabbath was not abrogated in the NT. It fails, however, to see the connectional fulfillment of the OT's Saturday observance in the NT's Sunday fulfillment. It also fails to understand God's progressive revelatory actions regarding the Sabbath and progressive revelation in general. The reformers particularly helped us to see how the Old Testament seventh day observance was a shadow fulfilled in Christ's resurrection on the Lord's Day (Sunday) (Col. 2:17). The OT Sabbath was not abrogated but rather fulfilled, for Jesus said, "*Do not think that I have come to abolish the*

Law or the Prophets; I have not come to abolish them but to fulfill them" (Mt. 5:17). The seventh day cycle would be preserved but on a different day. In other words, every seventh day would be observed as the Sabbath and the Sabbath Day concept would be maintained. Even still, we should note that this weekly Sabbath is an eschatological sign or pointer to the future rest which awaits those who have believed in Christ (Heb. 4:3,9) (Reymond 23). Dr. Richard Gaffin wisely remarks, "Scripture teaches that the weekly Sabbath was a creation ordinance and that it was given as the type par excellence of the eschatological state toward which creation is moving" (Gaffin 160). So, we must understand that as Christians observe the Sabbath, their observance points as a sign of eschatological (eschatology is the study of the last things) hope that one day they will rest in heaven with their God.

There is another view, **loose-sabbatarianism,** which holds that it doesn't matter which day Christians meet. This view is often characterized as viewing each day alike, leaving the observation of the Sabbath up to the individual without moral obligation. This view seems quite attractive at first glance for it portrays the appearance of biblical freedom in Christ. But the danger of loose-sabbatarianism is that it often disregards the reasons (as mentioned above) for Sabbath Day observance, and as a result, leads many Christians to flippantly ignore the significance of the Sabbath at all. Many believers have embraced this view as a result of misinterpreting the following key passages: Rom. 14:5-6, Gal. 4:9-10, and Col. 2:16-17. These passages have been taken to mean that a Sabbath Day observance is no longer obligatory. Since these passages are so significant, let us seek to briefly explain their meaning for clarification.

Romans 14:5-6 is an often-used passage by loose-sabbatarians. It should be noted that one of the main purposes of the book of Romans is to establish a proper understanding of how Jews and Gentiles are to relate to one another. Judaism was filled with ceremonial food laws and religious days that were observed in addition to the Sabbath Day.

It seems most contextually correct to interpret Rom. 14:5 as addressing the commonly held view that "the holy days of the ceremonial economy" had "abiding sanctity" (Murray 177-78). Paul obviously is referring to the ceremonial Jewish food laws in the preceding four verses. This context, therefore, should lead us to understand that verse 5 and 6 are referring to similar ceremonial days; not the Sabbath Day. Since Paul was willing to accommodate his weaker Jewish brothers, he allows them to continue their ceremonial observances, with the stipulation that they mustn't require the Gentiles to observe them. Paul calls both groups to make sure that their conscious decisions are made under the Lordship of Christ (Ro. 14:7-8) which will "*lead to peace and mutual edification*" (Rom. 14:19). Perhaps Paul was more lenient here in allowing the continuance of Jewish ceremonialisms because heretical views between the Jews and Gentiles were not as extensive in the church at Rome as they were in the church at Galatia (Gal. 4:9-10) and Colossae (Col. 2:16-17). We should remember that the Jewish ceremonial laws were fulfilled in the person of Christ and therefore rendered non-obligatory. Thus, since this passage seems to point to how to deal with the ceremonial law (i.e. special days, food laws, etc.), it shouldn't be applied to the Sabbath Day at all. Therefore, Sabbath Day observance is not hindered by this passage.

Another important passage is **Galatians 4:9-10**. Some interpreters have used this passage to denounce the observance of a Sabbath Day obligation. Like the passage above, this text must be interpreted in the light of its context. We should recognize that Paul was combating Judaizers that had infiltrated the churches of Galatia (Gal. 2:14-16). They were destroying the pure gospel by adding legalistic requirements for salvation. Paul would have no one add to Christ since He was the only means of salvation. To do otherwise would have placed all humanity back under the slavery of the law. With this in mind, we can see that such legalistic requirements such as special days, months, seasons, and years would have made void the grace of God. These ceremonial observances were meant to be carried out under the old Israelite economy, but met their fulfillment in the person of Christ (Col. 2:17). Paul is not attacking a Sabbath Day observance but rather legalistic ceremonial obligations. Now that we have looked at two very important texts, we mustn't forget Col. 2:16-17, possibly the most controversial text in our discussion of the Sabbath.

Colossians 2:16-17 is frequently used by loose-sabbatarians to support their position. It is interesting that this is the only place in Paul's epistles where the word Sabbath occurs. Again, it is important to note the context in order to properly interpret the passage. Paul was attacking a type of incipient gnosticism that had syncretized (joined together) elements of Judaism, Gentile mysticism, and Christianity. It is most evident throughout the letter that some false teachers were teaching that Christ was not enough for the full Christian experience. Such teachers were requiring the additional experience of visions, ascetic behavior, and Jewish ceremonial obligations in order to experience what was considered to be a "fuller Christianity". This idea of adding to the person and work of Christ was not new to Paul. He had dealt with a similar problem in his letter to the Galatians. This passage again seems to be dealing with the ceremonial laws and additional Gentile observances. When we look more carefully at the Greek form for the word "Sabbath" in verse 16, it seems to open up more clearly the meaning of the text. The Greek word sabbatōn is a plural noun that can either be rendered "sabbaths" or "sabbath days". The New International Version and the New American Standard Bible translations are a bit misleading since they translate this word as a single "*Sabbath day*". Actually, the King James Version is a better translation here (i.e. "*the sabbath days*") and the New King James Version is even better (i.e. "*sabbaths*"). This is very important because this word in the overall context should not be interpreted as referring to the "Sabbath Day." It should rather be understood as pointing to additional Jewish sabbath days, "since Lev. 23 and Numbers 29 make it clear that the Jews called many of their festivals Sabbaths (cf. particularly Lev. 23:32 with reference to the Day of Atonement)" (Rayburn 84). Therefore, we should conclude that Paul was not talking about the "Sabbath Day," but was rather speaking about other festival days that were being considered obligatory. Such festival days were part of the Jewish ceremonial laws of the OT. For Paul, such ceremonial sabbaths were fulfilled in Christ and were no longer obligatory. In no way was Paul speaking against the Sabbath Day specified in the Fourth Commandment. The theologian, Dr. Robert Rayburn, describes Paul's intentions well: "He was instructing believers not to attach special significance and sacredness to Jewish religious festivals and thus to pass judgment on those who failed to observe them, but rather to rejoice in their wonderful new-found liberty in Christ" (Rayburn 84).

I suggest a third position known as the **semi-sabbatarian** view, which is the view that most Christians throughout church history have embraced. This view is, "essentially the same as strict sabbatarianism but transfers its demands from Saturday, the seventh day, to Sunday, the first day of the week" (Harm 963). This position suits best the progressive revelatory nature of Scripture. There are many reasons why it should be considered the most valid position: (1) Sunday was the day in which the Lord rose from the dead and His resurrection became the heart of the gospel (eg. Acts 2:31; 4:2,10, 33; Rom. 10:9; I Cor. 15:4). (2) Sunday best represents God's eternal Sabbath in that it reminds believers of their eternal Sabbath in Christ (Heb. 4:3). In Christ's resurrection day we have the reality in which the Old Testament Saturday Sabbath was a shadow (Col. 2:17). The work of Christ fulfilled the law and thus in Him the Sabbath reached its fulfillment (Mt. 5:17). (3) The first day of the week became a normative assembly time and worship day amongst Jewish and Gentile believers after Christ's resurrection (Acts 20:7; I Cor. 16:2; Rev. 1:10). (4) After the New Testament era, early Christians still considered Sunday to be the day of worship (Didache 14:1; Justin, First Apology 67:3) (Young 1043). (5) The pouring out of the Holy Spirit occurred on Pentecost (Acts 2) which was the first day of the week. (6) It seems quite clear that Sunday observance was given apostolic sanction by Paul. Lowery notes that Paul "also directed the Corinthian church to make their contribution to the collection for the needy on a Sunday (1 Cor. 16:2), a practice which likely, though not necessarily, coincided with the meeting of the church" (Lowery 649). (7) The apostle John sanctioned the "Lord's Day" (a Sunday) as the day in which he received his revelation. The way in which he uses this term without defining it further implies that this day was widely recognized amongst Christians to be a special day. One author points out that the Roman word "Sunday" (which first appears in Justin's writings, First Apology 67.3) was gradually replaced by the Christian phrase "The Lord's Day" and was widely used throughout the Roman empire (Lowery 648). (8) Finally, we should greatly consider the weight of Christian tradition which has observed the Sabbath on the first day of the week ever since the conception of the early church.

We see clear evidence of the early practice of the church meeting on Sunday in the comments of the second century church father Justin Martyr who said, "And on the day called Sunday, all who live in cities or in the country gather together to one place, and the memoirs of the apostles or the writings of the prophets are read...But Sunday is the day on which we all hold our common assembly, because it is the first day on which God, having wrought a change in the darkness and matter, made the world; and Jesus Christ our Savior on the same day rose from the dead" (Justin Martyr's First Apology, Chapter 67). Dr. Morton Smith confirms the church's Lord's Day observance by quoting the eminent church historian Dr. Philip Schaff who said, "Nothing short of apostolic precedence can account for the universal religious observance (of the Lord's day) in the churches of the second century. There is no dissenting voice (Church History, Vol. II, p. 201)" (Smith 7). All the above reasons should lead us to conclude that Sunday is the Christian Sabbath and, therefore, should be faithfully observed. The question now arises as to how should we observe this day?

4 | HOW SHOULD WE OBSERVE THE SABBATH DAY?

You may at this point in our study be expressing a sigh of relief: "finally we're getting to the practical stuff." It may disappoint you that I'm not going to provide a long a list of *dos* and *don'ts*. The most important thing that we need to realize is that our Sabbath Day observance must be motivated by God's grace; not from some desire to earn favor with our Lord. When we consider how we must observe the Sabbath, our starting point must begin with the Lord of the Sabbath.

The Lord of the Sabbath

Christ calls all people to rest in Him. In order to properly honor the Lord's Day, we must first embrace Jesus Christ, the one who has given us this precious day. Otherwise, it will become nothing but a legalistic requirement, rather than a delight. Legalism is a view that teaches that we can earn a right standing with God by following His law. The Christian, however, is to be motivated by the love of Christ and the grace of God (Eph. 2:8-10; 2 Cor. 5:14). Jesus says, *"Come to me, all you who are weary and burdened and I will give you rest"* (Matthew 11:28). If you have never invited Christ into your heart as your Savior and Lord, I encourage you to do so right now. Jesus will give your soul present and eternal rest (Mt. 11:29) and cleanse you from all your sins. Everyone must receive Him into their hearts in order to be saved (John 1:12). Please take the time right now to confess your sins to Jesus and ask Him to forgive you of all your sins. According the Scriptures, He died for your sins on the cross and rose from the dead on the first day of the week (the Christian Sabbath) (see 1 Cor. 15:3-4). Please place your trust in Him as your Savior and Lord. If you do so with sincerity, Jesus promises that He will give you peace and rest for your soul (Mt. 11:29; John 6:47). Here's a suggested prayer that millions of Christians have prayed in some form over the centuries to accept Christ:

> *"Lord Jesus Christ, I know I am a sinner and do not deserve eternal life. But, I believe You died and rose from the grave to purchase a place in heaven for me. Lord Jesus, please come into my life; take control of my life; forgiven my sins and save me. I repent of my sins and now place my trust in you for my salvation. I accept the free gift of eternal life. Amen"*
> (Evangelism Explosion International 17).

If you have prayed this prayer, welcome to the family of God! I encourage you to find a Bible-believing church and to start attending its Sunday worship services (see Acts 2:42-47; Heb. 10:24-25). Tell the pastor or church leaders what you have done and ask for help in growing as a new Christian. If you have truly trusted in Christ, the Lord of the Sabbath, then you are well on your way to properly observing His day of rest.

Avoid the Extremes

Before we look at what God desires for us to do on the Sabbath, we need to be mindful that there are extreme views that should be avoided. Bruce A. Ray has wisely noted, "Two equally great and destructive dangers that we must avoid when talking about the Sabbath are legalism and lawlessness" (Ray 28).

The Pharisees (the Jewish religious leaders of Jesus' day) had a huge list of *dos* and *don'ts* that they required people to observe on the Sabbath. Centuries prior and up to the time of Christ, the Jewish religious leaders formulated many rules which were largely oral tradition, created to serve as a hedge around the OT law. As a result, **a legalistic spirit**, instead of an attitude of grace, dominated the Jewish religious establishment by the time of Christ. We see an example of this legalistic spirit in one of Jesus' encounters with the Pharisees. Jesus saw a man who had been an invalid for thirty-eight years (Jn. 5:5). In His compassion, He healed the man and the Pharisees responded by quickly accusing Jesus of breaking the Sabbath. The Scriptures tell us that Jesus told the man, *"Get up! Pick up your mat and walk,"* and he immediately was healed. The man at once picked up his mat and walked. The Jews then reacted with a legalistic response by telling the man, *"It is the Sabbath; the law forbids you to carry your mat"* (Jn. 5:11).

A strong oral tradition, made up of teaching by rabbis and elders, promoted the idea that God's people must follow legalistic requirements in order to become righteous. This legalistic tradition, held in Christ's day, can be seen clearly in the teachings of the Jewish Talmud, a collection of oral Rabbinic teaching that was written no earlier than AD 200.

Bruce Ray further illustrates this legalistic tradition by stating, "The tractate entitled *Shabbath* in the Talmud lists thirty-nine categories of work that are prohibited on the Sabbath. Each one of these categories is further subdivided into thirty-nine sections, making over 1,500 rules and regulations that one who would be righteous must keep" (Ray 66). This was a tremendous burden on the people. Even the Pharisees couldn't keep all these regulations. Ray further comments about this legalistic mountain by stating, "it was forbidden to unfasten a button, cut your toenails, or carry anything heavier than a dried fig. A man could not wear false teeth, because if they fell out, he would have to carry them, and that would be work. A tailor could not carry a needle in his pocket on the Sabbath because that was one of the tools of his trade, so carrying it would be work" (Ray 66). We, too, need to be careful not to fall into the same trap of the Pharisees, who commanded others to follow manmade rules on the Sabbath. God's people must avoid legalism.

There is another spiritually dangerous view that we must avoid when thinking about the Sabbath. It is **the notion that we can do anything we want on the Sabbath**. One man told me, "I don't need to go to church on Sunday. I'd rather go fishing somewhere than go to some worship service. Besides, I'm closer to God when I'm out on my favorite lake." Although fishing is one of my favorite hobbies, I cannot agree with this man's perspective. Fishing, or anything else that we decide to do, must not become our first priority when thinking about the Christian Sabbath. Too often our society gives in to the idea that by first doing what we want to do, we will experience fulfillment. Personal pleasure has become an idol that many bow down to in worship. This does not mean that following God's Will does not bring us pleasure, for I believe that it ultimately will. But the truth is that when we put God's Will first before our own, it is then that we will experience a godly pleasure that is in keeping with His Word (Js. 1:25; 1 John 1:5; 2 Tim. 3:4; Heb. 11:25).

Sunday is not a day in which we can choose to do anything we want to do. Many people today would rather follow their own will on the Lord's Day than the Lord's Will. This loose and flippant interpretation of the Christian Sabbath presents a problem: it is inconsistent with the Bible's teaching that Christians are called to follow the law of God (Jn. 14:15, 21,23). Many theologians call this loose view "licentiousness." Those who hold to this understanding of the Sabbath believe that they have the license to do whatever they please on Sundays. Licentiousness, of course, will sooner or later get Christians into a lot of trouble, not only on the Sabbath, but on other days of the week. Therefore, it is vital that we recognize the Lord's call to follow His Will; not ours (Mt. 6:10).

The Right Attitude

A church member once expressed, "I feel like the Sabbath is not really a restful time for me. I'm so busy on the Lord's Day that it feels like a burden rather than a blessing."

My heart goes out to this dear Christian. But what is the solution? First, we need to change our attitude and thinking about the Sabbath. God really wants us to delight in it, not find it a drudgery. We need to think about what the day means and why God has given it to us. It is especially important that parents help their children to see the Sabbath as a joyful experience. Joseph Pipa remarks, "If we want our children to love the Sabbath, we must make the day a delight for them" (Pipa 184).

God truly wants us to have a joyful and refreshing experience on the Sabbath. He desires for us to have the same attitude as my son, Micah, who often tells me, "I love Sunday!" We need to remember that the Sabbath is a gift of God's grace. It is a day in which we especially ponder the mercies of God to us in Christ; a time set aside to help us grow closer to God and His people. Micah looks forward each week to the Lord's Day. He tells me, "Dad, I like Sunday because I learn about Jesus and get to see my Christian friends." His childlike excitement is a taste of how we all should look forward to the Sabbath. If we find ourselves becoming overburdened with certain Sabbath activities, perhaps we need to cut back a bit. By no means, however, should we cut back on the corporate worship of God (Heb. 10:23-26). But, we may need to reassess why we are so involved in our various Sabbath activities.

Our ultimate motivation for Sabbath observance should not be guilt, but our love for Christ and the grace that He has given. We need to remember that God doesn't call us to be busy on the Sabbath, but rather to rest in Him. Along with the Psalmist, we should look at the Sabbath with joy and make it our delight. May this Sabbath Psalm encourage you in your attitude toward the Lord's Day: "*It is good to praise the Lord and make music to your name, O Most High, to proclaim your love in the morning and your faithfulness at night, to the music of the ten-stringed lyre and the melody of the harp. For you make me **glad** by your deeds, O Lord; I sing for **joy** at the works of your hands. How great are your works, O Lord, how profound your thoughts!*" (Psalm 92:1-5).

The Right Principles

We have been cautioned against the extreme views concerning the Sabbath, but now we must turn to what God requires of us on this Holy Day. The answer as to how we should exactly observe the Sabbath is somewhat subjective, but there are various biblical teachings that provide God's people with helpful guidelines and principles to follow. First of all, the scriptures teach us to **regularly observe the Sabbath** (Dt. 5:12; Heb. 10:24). Our Lord Himself provides us with an example of regular Sabbath keeping (Lk. 4:16). We are to allow the Sabbath to become our day of "rest." This cannot mean complete cessation of all activity or idleness since this is not the nature of God's rest (Gen. 2:2-3; Jn. 5:17). It is a spiritual, mental, and physical setting apart of this holy day and a "concentrated adoration of the Triune God" (Reymond 19). Dr. Reymond helps us to understand more clearly what "rest" means: namely, "the involvement in new, in the sense of different, activity. It means the cessation of the labor of the six days and the taking up of different labors appropriate to the Lord's Day" (Reymond 19).

In the enjoyment of the Sabbath, **believers are not to cause others to stumble** in leading them to profane the Sabbath (Ex. 20:8-11; 23:12). We are to give those who are dependent upon us the same opportunity to rest from their labor just as we are resting. Moses clearly makes this point in Dt. 5:13-14 where he says, *"(13) Six days you shall labor and do all your work, (14) but the seventh day is a Sabbath to the Lord your God. On it you shall not do any work, neither you, nor your son or daughter, nor your manservant or maidservant, nor your ox, your donkey or any of your animals, nor the alien within your gates, so that your manservant and maidservant may rest, **as you do**."*

The Sabbath is also meant as **a time for worship, mutual fellowship, and encouragement** with other believers (Heb. 10:25). Early Christian services provide us with elements which we should seek to emulate in our own Christian services, such as: the singing of psalms, hymns, and spiritual songs, the offering of prayers, the use of spiritual gifts, the reading of Scripture, the preaching and teaching of the Word, the taking of offerings for diaconal needs, and the proper administration of the sacraments (Acts 20:7; I Cor. 11:20-22; 14:26; 16:2; Col. 3:16).

Furthermore, it is important to **prepare for the Sabbath**. When God provided manna from heaven for the Israelites, He instructed them to prepare for the Sabbath by collecting a double portion of manna on the sixth day (Exodus 16:5). Some people frequently complain that they have trouble staying awake during Sunday morning worship services. Why is this? Usually it is because they have not prepared themselves for worship by getting enough sleep the night before. It is important that we prepare ahead of time for the Lord's Day, so that we will not feel pressured to profane it. The Lord Himself is a good example of one who makes preparations ahead of time for upcoming situations. This is the doctrine of Providence. God wants His children to imitate His behavior as much as possible (Eph. 5:1). Therefore, we should prepare for the Christian Sabbath.

Our observance, in addition, should exclude any worldly employments and recreations (Ex. 16:23-29; Isa. 58:13; Neh. 13:15-22). The Prophet Isaiah encourages us to avoid doing what we want to do on the Sabbath and instructs us to honor it. This implies that we should **seek to do what is pleasing to the Lord** on the Sabbath. God teaches us this principle when He says to Israel, *"(13) If you keep your feet from breaking the Sabbath and from doing **as you please** on my holy day, if you call the Sabbath a delight and the Lord's holy day honorable, and if you honor it by not going **your own way** and not doing **as you please** or speaking idle words, (14) then you will find your joy in the Lord, and I will cause you to ride on the heights of the land and to feast on the inheritance of your father Jacob. The mouth of the Lord has spoken"* (Isaiah 58:13-14).

The ministry of the Word and prayer are likewise vitally important on the Lord's Day. So, if you teach a Sunday school class or share the gospel with someone, you are doing something pleasing to the Lord (Luke 4:14-21; 13:10-17; Acts 2:1, 36-41; Acts 6:4; Eph. 6:18). Some people set aside a special time for prayer to God on the Lord's Day, since they have a bit more time on Sunday than the other days of the week. Many churches will have teams of people go out on a Sunday afternoon to share the gospel with their community. There are endless possibilities that the church can undertake in ministering the Word on the Christian Sabbath.

On the Lord's Day, the time we spend outside of corporate and private worship of God can also be taken up with **works of necessity** (I Sam. 21:6; Mt. 12:1; Mk. 2:23-28; Lk. 13:15; Lk. 14:5) and **mercy** (Mt. 12:7,8,11; Mk. 3:1-6). Hodge says it well: "And nothing is to be allowed to interfere with this consecration of the day except the evident and reasonable demands of necessity as far as our own interests are concerned, and of mercy as far as the necessities of our fellow-men and of dependent animals are concerned" (Hodge 283).

As we conclude our discussion on the right principles for Sabbath observance, perhaps the most clear and concise statement of the Bible's teaching on this matter is presented in the Westminster Confession of Faith. This beloved reformed confessional document was written in the 17th century and continues to help the church better understand the Scriptures. It states that:

> "*This Sabbath is then kept holy unto the Lord, when men, after a due **preparing** of their hearts, and **ordering** of their common affairs beforehand, do not only **observe an holy rest**, all the day, from their own works, words, and thoughts about their worldly employments and recreations, but also are taken up, the whole time, in the public and private exercises of His **worship**, and in the duties of **necessity** and **mercy**"* (Chapter 21, par. 8).

5 | SUMMARY

In summary, we have determined that the Sabbath is a perpetual creation ordinance and institution of God that has been grounded in the moral law. We have also seen that we should observe the Sabbath because God has commanded us to observe it and His commandment has not been abrogated (ended, annulled). It has been demonstrated that the OT Saturday Sabbath has been fulfilled in the NT Sunday Sabbath, which finds its reality in the person and work of Christ, particularly His resurrection. Furthermore, we have been encouraged to see our Sabbath rest as a sign of hope that we, as God's children, will one day experience our blessed rest in heaven. Finally, numerous suggestions have been given regarding how to observe the Sabbath in a manner that is both glorifying to God and edifying to ourselves and others. May the Sabbath become your precious day of delight, as you glory in it and seek to observe it as one who has truly found rest in Christ.

6 | STUDY QUESTIONS

📖 **Suggestion**: These study questions can be broken up into several lessons dealing with the Christian Sabbath?

1. What is the general attitude in the culture and church today concerning the Sabbath?

2. When did God institute the Sabbath & why (read Genesis 2:2-3; Exodus 20:8-11)?

3. What does the word Sabbath mean (see chapter 1)?

4. Can you name three reasons why the Sabbath should be observed (see chapter 2)? Explain.

5. Why do Christians practice their Sabbath on Sunday rather than on Saturday (see chapter 3)?

6. What are three views of the Sabbath (see chapter 3)? Please explain.

7. How are the following passages often misinterpreted: Romans 14:5-6; Gal. 4:9-10; and Col. 2:16-17 (see chapter 3)?

8. According to God's Word, how should we observe the Sabbath (see chapter 4)?

9. What are some things we could do to prepare ourselves for the Lord's Day?

10. In what way does Christ's resurrection affect your view of the Sabbath?

11. How does the Sabbath bring you joy (see pgs. 24-25)?

12. What were the circumstances that led you to rest in Christ, the Lord of Sabbath?

13. Why might it be significant to think of the Christian Sabbath as "the Lord's Day" versus "my day?"

14. How can we apply the pattern of Sabbath rest in the Lord to the other six days of the week? Elaborate.

15. Have you been challenged in your personal practice and understanding of the Sabbath? Explain.

Closing Prayer:

Ask God for His grace to help you apply specifically what He has taught you and to gently share it with others.

SCRIPTURE INDEX

Genesis
2:2-3, *6, 12, 24, 28*
2:3, *6*

Exodus
16:5, *25*
16:23-29, *25*
16:26, *7*
20, *7*
20:8ff., *8*
20:8-11, *7, 10, 24, 28*
23:12, *24*
31:13, *9*
31:17, *9*

Leviticus
23, *16*
23:32, *16*

Numbers
29, *16*

Deuteronomy
5:12-15, *9, 10*
5:12, *24*
5:13-14, *24*
5:15, *9*

1 Samuel
21:6, *26*

Nehemiah
13:15-22, *12, 25*

Psalms
92:1-5, *23*

Isaiah
56:2-8, *12*
58:13-14, *12, 25*
58:13, *25*

Jeremiah
17:27, *12*

Ezekiel
20:12, *9*
20:13, *9, 12*
20:20, *9, 10*

Matthew
5:17-20, *11, 14*
5:17, *14, 17*
6:10, *22*
11:28, *19*
11:29, *9, 19-20*
12:1, *26*
12:7-8, *26*
12:11, *26*

Mark
2:23-28, *26*
2:27, *8, 11*
3:1-6, *26*

Luke
4:14-21, *26*
4:16, *24*
13:10-17, *26*
13:15, *26*
14:5, *26*

John
1:12, *19*
5:5, *21*
5:11, *21*

5:17, *24*
6:47, *20*
14:15, *22*
14:21, *22*
14:23, *22*

Acts
2, *17*
2:1, *26*
2:31, *17*
2:36-41, *26*
2:42-47, *20*
4:2, *17*
4:10, *17*
4:33, *17*
6:4, *26*
20:7, *17, 25*

Romans
10:9, *17*
14:5-6, *14-15, 28*
14:5, *15*
14:7-8, *15*
14:19, *15*

1 Corinthians
11:20-22, *25*
12, *10*
14, *10*
14:26, *25*
15:3-4, *20*
15:4, *17*
16:2, *17, 18, 25*

2 Corinthians
5:14, *19*

Galatians
2:14-16, *15*
4:9-10, *14, 15-16, 28*

Ephesians
2:8-10, *19*
5:1, *25*
6:18, *26*

Colossians
2:16-17, *14, 15, 16-17, 28*
2:17, *13, 16, 17*
3:16, *25*

2 Timothy
3:4, *22*

Hebrews
4:3, *10, 14, 17*
4:9, *14*
10:23-26, *23*
10:24-25, *20*
10:24, *24*
10:25, *24*
10:26, *10*
11:25, *22*

James
1:25, *22*

1 John
1:5, *22*

Revelation
1:10, *17*
14:9ff., *13*
14:13, *10*

WORKS CITED

W. Baur, W. Arndt and F.W. Gingrich, <u>A Greek-English Lexicon of the New Testament and Other Early Christian Literature</u>. 1979 ed.

Calvin, John. <u>Institutes of the Christian Religion</u>. Ed. John T. McNeil. Trans. Ford Lewis Battles. Philadelphia: Westminster, 1960.

Gaffin, Richard. "Calvin and the Sabbath." Fearn, Rossshire, Great Britain, Mentor, 1998.

Hamilton, Victor P. "Shabbat." <u>Theological Wordbook of the Old Testament</u>. Ed. R. Laird Harris, Gleason L. Archer, and Bruce K. Waltke. Vol. 2. Chicago: Moody Press, 1980.

Harm, F.R. "Sabbatarianism." <u>Evangelical Dictionary of Theology</u>. Ed. Walter A. Elwell. Grand Rapids: Baker Book House, 1984.

Hodge, A.A. <u>The Confession of Faith</u>. Edinburgh: The Banner of Truth Trust, 1958.

Hollady, William L. <u>A Concise Hebrew and Aramaic Lexicon of the Old Testament</u>. Grand Rapids: Eerdmans, 1988.

Lowery, D.K. "Lord's Day." <u>Evangelical Dictionary of Theology</u>. Ed. Walter A. Elwell. Grand Rapids: Baker Book House, 1984.

Murray, J. "The Epistle to the Romans." <u>The New International Commentary on the New Testament</u>. vol. 2 Michigan: Eerdmans, 1965.

Martyr, Justin. "First Apology." Printed in Philip Schaff's Early Church Fathers. Christian Classics Ethereal Library at Calvin College. www.ccel.org/fathers 2/.

Pipa, Joseph A. "The Lord's Day." Fearn, Scotland: Christian Focus, 1997. *I highly recommend that you especially read chapters 11-13 which provide many practical grace-centered ideas on observing the Sabbath.*

Rausch, D.A. "Sabbath." <u>Evangelical Dictionary of Theology</u>. Ed. Walter A. Elwell. Grand Rapids: Baker Book House, 1984.

Ray, Bruce A. "Celebrating the Sabbath." Phillipsburg: P&R Publishing, 2000. *This is a short read but very pastoral. Well worth your time.*

Rayburn, Robert G. "Should Christians Observe the Sabbath?" <u>Presbyterion</u>. 10.1-2 (1984): 72-86.

Reymond, Robert L. "Lord's Day Observance: Man's Proper Response to the Fourth Commandment." <u>Presbyterion</u>. 13.1 (1987): 7-23.

Smith, Morton H. "A Call For a Return to Sabbath Observance." Greenville: Greenville Presbyterian Seminary. Articles printed in The Bulletin of Greenville Presbyterian Theological Seminary from fall 1992 to spring 1993.

Stibbs, A.M. "Hebrews." <u>The New Bible Commentary: Revised</u>. Ed. D. Guthrie. Grand Rapids: Eerdmans, 1970.

Young, E.J. and Bruce, F.F. "Sabbath." <u>New Bible Dictionary</u>. Tyndale House, Wheaton, 1982.